Crazy Dogs
WITH HUMOR

Julia Williams

CRAZY DOGS WITH HUMOR

© 2023, Julia Williams.

All rights reserved. This book or any portion thereof may not be reproduced or used in any manner whatsoever without the express written permission of the publisher except for the use of brief quotations in a book review.

Print ISBN: 979-8-35093-279-9
eBook ISBN: 979-8-35093-280-5

Collie	1
Poodle	3
German Shepherd	5
Rottweiler	7
Boxer	9
Pointer	11
Great Dane	13
Dachshund	15
Bloodhound	17
Afghan hound	19
Labrador	21
Akita	23
Terrier	25
Whippet	27
Chihuahua	29
Spaniel	31
Sheep Dog	33
Saint Bernard	35
Basenji	37
Bull dog	39
Dalmatian	41

Collie

Hello! Let's go out and party. I have some good news for you. Can you guess what it is? You can guess by my party hat. I came to tell you that the party just started. First I want to say that **collies** originated from Scotland. They are smart with a pointed face and deep set eyes. Collies breed can fool you because they are fast learners. Collies are quite friendly and good with children. Come into a collie world and join the party. Collies breed are also a wonderful family pet. I promise you won't regret it.

Fool	Entertain	Celebrate	Done	Foolish
Quest	Fun	Over	Naive	Home
Event	Regret	Passive	Visit	Gathering
Sad	Show	Welcome	Party	Sorry

Behavior	Bright	Companion	Consoling	Character
Brilliant	Faithful	Delicate	Moral	Clever
Loyal	Emotional	Personality	Intelligent	Reliable
Responsive	Qualities	Quick	Trust	Sensitive

Poodle

Poodles are a breed originated in Germany. They are popular in many homes. Poodles were used as a watch dog and bark at any unusual sounds. They are extremely smart with a big heart. Their breed of dog is excellent water retrievers and they barks a lot. If you decide to have a poodle for your pet, consider their upkeep. Poodles can also be easily trained. Poodles are not great kennel dogs. Poodles like to be active and free. They are a little cuddly and enjoy being free to hang out with you. Poodles are dainty and cute groomed from their head to their feet. It can cost you plenty, to keep a poodle looking pretty.

Cute	Brush	Cage	Aware	Order
Dainty	Clean	Doghouse	Look	Neat
Delicate	Groom	Kennel	Reveal	Tidy
Neat	Sleek	Shelter	See	Together

Best	Cost	Bring-back	Good	Cuddly
Excellent	Expensive	Regain	Keep	Hug
Great	Pricey	Retrieve	Renew	Loving
Superb	Steep	Winner	Retain	Snuggle

German Shepherd

The **German Shepherd** is intelligent, loyal, and energetic. They enjoy their family and when left alone they struggle with being separated for a long period of time. They're not aggressive, but when the enemy comes they have the instinct to let you know that a stranger is around. Shepherds are open to meet strangers, if they are familiar and not a threat. The shepherd are courageous, noble, obedient, and a bit curious. Shepherds are usually large and muscular. They are family protectors and very good to have as a family pet.

Cope	Aggressive	Feelings	Energetic	Effort
Attacking	Hunch	Lively	Strive	Combative
Impulse	Spirited	Struggle	Offensive	Instinct
Strong	Tackle	Threatening	Urge	Zest
Guest	Gentle	Curious	Devoted	Intruder
Kind	Odd	Docile	Outsider	Highly
Peculiar	Faithful	Stranger	Humor	Strange
Loyal	Visitor	Noble	Wonder	Obedient

Rottweiler

Rottweilers are some crazy outrageous daring dogs. They help policeman do their jobs. Rottweilers are a breed that can be mean sometimes. Their shoulders are broad and fairly large. They are a breed that originated from Germany. They are built very strong. But don't get me wrong. They are built to protect their family at all times. Rottweilers are a breed that's good for a family pet. You can't go wrong if you decide to purchase a Rottweiler. They won't harm you. Rottweilers do more than just guard your home. They are eager to please you.

Anxious	Buy	Defend	Cop	Desire
Gain	Guard	Detective	Eager	Get
Patrol	Officer	Excitement	Pick-up	Protect
Patrolman	Interest	Purchase	Shield	Policeman

Broad	Crazy	Bold	Attack	Large
Funny	Brave	Damage	Muscle	Humorous
Daring	Destroy	Muscular	Nutty	Fearless
Harm	Wide	Stupid	Spunky	Hurt

Boxer

Boxers are a breed that's originated from Germany. Make no mistake they got their name fair and square. It doesn't matter what breed you like, never turn your back. Boxers are a family dog and they love children. Boxers can be very destructive if left alone for a long period of time. Boxers can grow to medium and large sizes with a large head. Boxers can live up to 10 years old. They are an intelligent breed of dog. They can learn very quickly. They have dark brown eyes and a black nose. Boxers can be a loyal pet to have around. Boxers are a breed of dog just doing their job.

Confusion	Around	Black	Boxer	Error
Change	Color	Fighter	Fault	Circle
Dark	Kick	Mistake	Rotate	Shade
Punch	Wrong	Turn	Skin	Slugger

Devoted	Damage	Especially	Bright	Faithful
Destructive	Exceedingly	Brilliant	Firm	Devastating
Extremely	Clever	Loyal	Fatal	Greatly
Intelligent	True	Harmful	Highly	Sharp

Pointer

You have found what you were looking for me! I knew you would find me here. **Pointers** are a hunting breed of dog they have no fear. A pointer breed originated from Spain. Pointers have no shame. They have long silky ears that lie on their cheeks. Pointers have a strong back and a long tail. If anyone ask you about a pointer, tell them that their breed is never aggressive. Pointers are truly well behaved with a strong will and very energetic. You will have to be healthy and strong enough to have a pointer breed around.

Creative	Catch	Bashful	Fearless	Developed
Fetch	Coy	Frighten	Discovered	Hunting
Embarrass	Phobia	Find	Search	Shame
Scared	Found	Uncover	Shy	Spooked

Alert	Adapt	Clever	Active	Awake
Adjusting	Creative	Aggressive	Aware	Alter
Expertise	Energetic	Lookout	Arrange	Genius
Lively	Watch	Fit	Talent	Motivated

Great Dane

Great Danes stand up straight and tall. Their chest are built broad and strong. Their legs are muscular and long. Great Danes ears stick up and never droop down. Danes have a smooth glossy coat, thick smooth hair and that's no joke. Great Danes are adaptable dogs. The Great Dane breed of dog is important for having great stability for their bravery. Danes are sociable, friendly, and eager to please. Danes also respond well to consistent training. Great Danes originated in Germany. They are a breed of dog that's one out of a million that live in most people homes. Would you like to have a breed like a Great Dane around? You can't go wrong.

Breast	Brawny	Gloss	Broad	Chest
Muscle	Polish	Bulky	Bust	Muscular
Slick	Chunky	Lumbar	Robust	Smooth
Heavy	Tit	Strong	Suave	Thick

Adaptable	Connection	Friendly	Solid	Adjustable
Consistent	Generous	Stability	Flexible	Comply
Kind	Stable	Skills	Regular	Pleasant
Supportive	Suitable	Sympathy	Sociable	Unbreakable

Dachshund

Have you ever imagined what's it like to go through a ring of fire? it's Hot! Hot! Hot! What a chance to take, you can't make one mistake. **Dachshunds** have a long shape body with short legs. Dachshunds are known as a wiener dog. They are known to be smart pets for their bravery. They originated in Germany to be hunting dogs. Dachshunds tends to bark a lot. They are sensitive to changing their environment which increase excessive barking. Dachshunds was used to fit into small holes that's the way it goes.

Blaze	Error	Bold	Cavity	Burn
Fault	Bravery	Decay	Fiery	Mistake
Courage	Holes	Flame	Regret	Fearless
Hollow	Hot	Wrong	Tough	Open

Climate	Beyond	Affect	Enlarge	Condition
Excessive	Detect	Greater	Environment	Extreme
Emotion	Growth	Lives	More	Increase
Sensitive	Natural	Overflow	Respond	Stretch

Bloodhound

Bloodhounds are a breed of dog that goes back to the middle ages. They hunt by scent and not by sight. Bloodhounds can follow your scent on dry land, even if you're on the run. I tell you that bloodhounds are a breed that was used in the 1800's to hunt down people that was on the run. Bloodhounds will stay on your trail, there's no way you can escape their keen sense of smell. You can't hide from a bloodhound. They're good with children and get along well with other animals. Bloodhounds like to chew on everything and anything. They are a breed that was used by law enforcement all across America.

Avoid	Century	Airy	Aim	Break
Generation	Fragrance	See	Escape	Middle-ages
Odor	Sight	Relief	Old-times	Scent
Vision	Run	Years	Smell	Power

Across	Chew	Comply	Authority	Cross-over
Crush	Enforce	Command	Opposite	Gnaw
Enforcement	Control	Overflow	Grind	Obedience
Direct	Pass	Nibble	Obey	Power

Afghan hound

The **Afghan** is known by its thick silky coat. They have the power to leap high and the ability to turn easily. They are very valuable with a special ability. Afghans are swift runners that makes them one of the best. They are sporting dogs that's found in Afghanistan. Afghans have a narrow head thick neck and silky fine fur. Afghans like to be brushed and groomed. They also have a wonderful personality. Would you like to have a pet awesome as that? having an Afghan for your family pet.

Brush	Fine	Behavior	Coarse	Glide
Silky	Character	Curve	Smooth	Strands
Feelings	Heavy	Strokes	Texture	Personality
Thick	Sweep	Thin	Thoughts	Thickness

Long	Ability	Greatness	Delightful	Narrow
Capable	Important	Gorgeous	Small	Powerful
Priceless	Lovely	Straight	Strength	Valuable
Marvelous	Thin	Strong	Worthy	Wonderful

Labrador

Labradors are a proud breed of dog. Their breed originated from Canada long time ago. Their head is wide and they have very strong teeth. Labradors prefer to be kept clean no matter what. Their eyes are usually black or brown. Labs are a British breed of dog that was developed in the United Kingdom for fishing. Labradors are usually friendly and out going. Their legs are straight and their tail are long. Having a Labrador you can't go wrong.

Bring-back	Custom	Fair	Broad	Fetch
Habit	Large	Larger	Recover	Normal
Medium	Oversize	Regain	Same	Size
Wide	Retriever	Usually	Small	Width

Boast	Beginning	Admire	Direct	Glad
Developed	Favor	Even	Honored	Originated
Like	In-line	Pleased	Rise	Offer
Non-stop	Proud	Up-rise	Prefer	Straight

Akita

Akitas are a spiritual breed of dog. They were presented at the birth of a child. When a person was sick, an Akita was there to express health and happiness. Akitas are large and powerful with a big neck, wide chest, and a curled up tail. They have button shaped eyes and strong legs. Akitas are a historic breed of dog. Akitas breed originated from the mountain of northern Japan. They even have a fun side. You can't tell by looking at their face. Akita's breed is as good as it gets.

Express	Incredible	Feature	Curve	Emotion
Powerful	Inform	Pointed	Felt	Strength
Introduce	Round	Speak	Strong	Presented
Shape	Style	Superb	Show	Straight
Care	Event	Height	Arise	Fitness
History	Highest	Become	Health	Historical
Mountain	Developed	Medical	Important	Peak
Originated	Physical	Past	Tall	Started

Terrier

What do you think of me? Do you like my attire? I am dressed this way to impress you. **Terriers** will be the first to alert you from harm or danger. Their breed is always up to playing games and being adventurous. They originated from England. Terriers also love to learn. Terriers need an outlet for their extreme energy. Their face is long and straight fast powerful and safe. Terriers have a keen sense of smell and a natural born swimmer. But by looking at them you just can't tell.

Adventurous	Alert	Active	Line	Daring
Aware	Aware	Sharp	Ideas	Careful
Forceful	Stiffness	Involving	Observe	Powerful
Straight	Risk	Watch	Work	Unbend

Adore	Impress	Human	Sense	Attire
Pretty	Nature	Sight	Clothes	Remember
Natural	Smell	Dress	Show	Real
Taste	Garment	Smart	Relate	Touch

Whippet

Whippets are a different breed of dogs. They hunt by sent not by sight. Whippets originated from England and was used for a racing dog. Whippets are the speediest of all dogs, and they're strong and lean, but never mean. They have very few health problems. Whippets are very alert and they are well known that's why whippets never give up on a race. They are a gentle breed of dog who love to chase. Whippets need to have a good run around, they also love to cuddle up on the couch.

Different	Chase	Complete	Alarm	Opposite
Hunt	Drag	Alert	Separated	Search
Game	Aware	Unique	Snipe	Race
Caution	Unlike	Track	Run	Ready

Daybed	Gentle	Chase	Able	Couch
Kind	Follow	Capable	Futon	Nice
Hunt	Clever	Love seat	Pleasant	Pursuit
Skillful	Sofa	Tender	Trail	Talent

Chihuahua

Look at me! Do you like what you see? I like you. I am a **chihuahua** small in size. My ears and tail stick straight up and never droop down. Chihuahua breed originated from Mexico, there they got their name. Chihuahua is a breed that's diminutive in size. They are known as a toy dog. Chihuahuas are also easy to train and very obedient. These breeds of dogs burn three time as many calories as other canines by being so active. That's what causes the shivering and shaking as a side effect. If you believe in a chihuahua breed of dog. Remember it's always fun to have a chihuahua for your pet.

Canine	Carbs	Effect	Mexico	Dingo
Calories	Event	Mexican	Dog	Energy
Outcome	Gulf	Mutt	Fats	Result
Pablo	Pup	Measure	Succeed	Spanish

Attentive	Diminutive	Shaking	Stick	Complaint
Little	Nervous	Clever	Devoted	Petite
Quiver	Cling	Faithful	Small	Tremble
Glue	Obedient	Tiny	Uneasy	Lock

Spaniel

Spaniels were once described as a woodcock prized hunting companion. Loyal and charming, faithful and mostly unique. Spaniels are the most popular that's known in the world. They also have been in many movies and shows. The spaniel was originated in Spain but, the most modern breeds were developed in Britain. They are a breed of dog that's nice to have around. Spaniels need to be brushed regularly to keep their coat smooth. They are a nice breed for your family pet.

Woodcock	Admire	Delivery	Glorious	Sandpiper
Cherished	Help	Honored	Seagulls	Dear
Presented	Noble	Tringa	Favorite	Service
Outstanding	Turn stone	Prized	Serving	Respected

Fresh	Conquer	Devoted	Developed	Latest
Prevail	Loyal	Enlarge	Modern	Succeed
Steadfast	Evolve	Stylish	Victory	True
Expand	Leading	Win-back	Trusting	Grow

Sheep Dog

Sheep dogs are great companions for children. They are cute and very lovable. Sheep dogs were used as a watch dog. They enjoy children and likes a loving home. When you see a sheep dog, it's hard to resist them. Their breed are hairy from their head to tail. If you purchase a sheep dog as a puppy, try to train them everyday while they are young. Sheep dogs faces are covered in fur. When you look them in the face you can barely see their eyes. They are so shaggy that every part is covered except their pink little tongue and black nose is the only thing revealed.

Champion	Affection	Coarse	Defeat	Defender
Kind	Furry	Define	Fighter	Lovable
Shaggy	Resist	Warrior	Precious	Tangled
Submit	Winner	Sweet	Woolly	Surrender

Belief	Careful	Buy	Child	Confidence
Gently	Bold	Lively	Firm	Gradually
Obtain	Off-spring	Pride	Increase	Pick-up
Young	Rely	Slowly	Purchase	Youth

Saint Bernard

I am proud of being me! Known as a **Saint Bernard** you see. Bernard's help save and set free. Bernards are very strong with a sure face. Bernard's originated from Europe. Bernard's job is very important. They rescue people from harm. Bernard's are gentle and known to rarely bark at strangers. Their face are calm and peaceful. They are loving gentle and cuddly. Saint Bernard's moves with quickness and swiftness. It's hard to own a breed like a Bernard with their generosity.

Happy	Calm	Bring	Friendly	Honor
Focus	Deliver	Generosity	Please	Okay
Fetch	Kind	Proud	Peace	Rescue
Open-hand	Satisfy	Slow	Retrieve	Unselfishness
Aggressive	Chatty	Caress	Gentle	Attack
Gossip	Cuddle	Nice	Forceful	Mouthy
Huggable	Pleasant	Hostility	Talkative	Kissable
Soft	Offensive	Wordy	Lovable	Tender

Basenji

You may already know that a Basenji breed is not that popular around. They are known as a bark-less African hound. **Basenji** is not entirely mute, they are a very smart breed of dog. Basenji have a wonderful personality and can be difficult to train sometimes, if they choose not to obey you. Basenji make sounds and get their point across. Their breed can be notable rare. Basenji breed of dog originated in ancient Egypt. Their forehead is wrinkled their tail is small and tight but, where they are from that's alright.

Great	Creased	Bold	Accepted	Important
Fold	Demand	Carry-out	Notable	Lined
Difficult	Obey	Out-standing	Wrinkle	Touch
Take	Remarkable	Wrinkly	Trouble	Trouble

Accepted	Bark-less	Edge	Breed	Fashion
Mute	End	Gender	Favorite	Quiet
Point	Mixed	Popular	Silent	Sharp
Pure	Suitable	Speechless	Tip	Trait

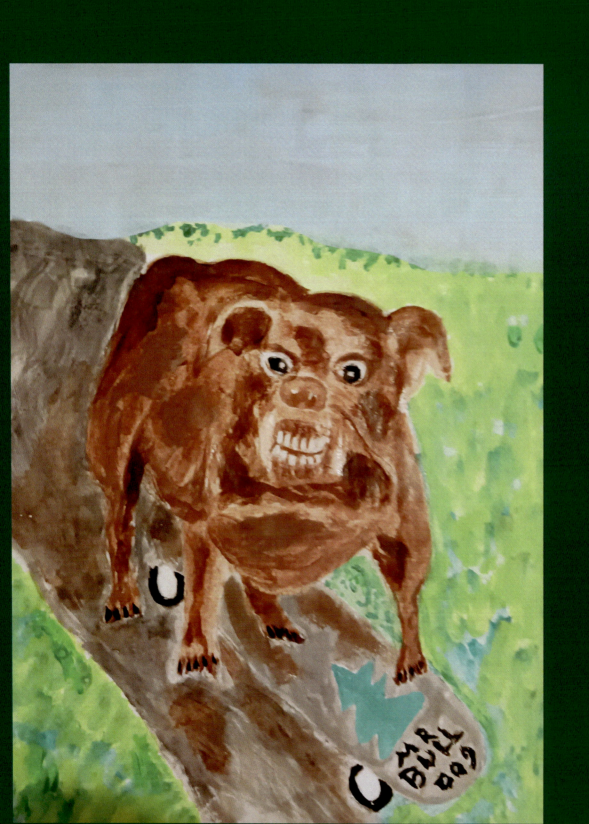

Bull dog

Here is something new for you. **Bull dogs** are remarkably smart with a great big heart. Bull dogs don't mean you any harm, they know how to have fun. Bull dogs are a breed of dog that originated from England. They are a hefty dog with a wrinkled up face and a pushed in nose. They are involved in fewer incidents than you would expect. Their breed need to be sociable starting at an early age. Bull dogs enjoy eating regularly everyday. They're not cheap to maintain in their daily life. They can be aggressive and a little mean sometimes. Bull dogs like to have fun with their owner by having fun riding and sliding together.

Aware	Emotion	Able	Amusing	Discover
Feeling	Bright	Enjoyable	New	Heart
Intelligent	Exciting	Recent	Love	Smart
Fun	Seen	Tenderness	Wise	Witty

Heavy	Affair	Enjoy	Aggressive	Husky
Episode	Friendly	Combative	Large	Event
Gathering	Forceful	Powerful	Happening	Involved
Hostility	Strong	Incident	Sociable	Offensive

Dalmatian

Dalmatian are a breed of dog that's unique, with black or brown spots. They was used mainly as a carriage dog. Their skull is wide long and flat on top. Dalmatians was used as a hunting dog, having a strong instinct for hunting. Dalmatians are friendly and a delightful breed of dog. They was also used as a coach dog. Dalmatians also helped policeman do their jobs. If you purchase a Dalmatian breed I tell you that they are not cheap. Dalmatians have a lot of energy and can run for miles. It's just a Dalmatian style.

Beautiful	Carrying	Bought	Instinct	Charming
Coach	Buy	Impulse	Friendly	Delivery
Purchase	Conscious	Honest	Transport	Pay
Mood	Delightful	Wagon	Spend	Response

Bargain	Energy	Behavior	Brain	Cheap
Lively	Design	Cranial	Cheaper	Powerful
Expression	Head	Low-price	Spirited	Fashion
Organ	Reduce	Tough	Style	Skull